LEWES
IN OLD PHOTOGRAPHS

A GROUP OF WORKERS AND OFFICIALS pose at Lewes Race Course in 1874. The new course was officially opened on 15 April 1874.

LEWES
IN OLD PHOTOGRAPHS

COLLECTED BY
JUDY MIDDLETON

ALAN SUTTON

Alan Sutton Publishing Limited
Phoenix Mill · Far Thrupp · Stroud · Gloucestershire

First Published 1990

British Library Cataloguing in Publication Data

Lewes in old photographs.
1. East Sussex. Lewes, history
I. Middleton, Judy
942.257

ISBN 0-86299-761-5

Typeset in 9/10 Korinna
Typesetting and origination by
Alan Sutton Publishing Limited
Printed in Great Britain by
Dotesios Printers Limited

CONTENTS

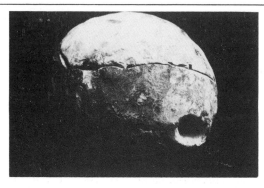

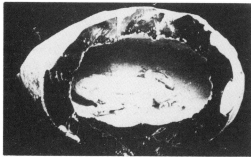

AN OLD POSTCARD of the famous 'Toad in the Hole'. The flint nodule was found in 1898 near Lewes by Thomas Nye and Joseph Isted. Because the flint was light in weight for its size, Thomas Nye cut it open and the mummified toad was found inside.

INTRODUCTION

The view from the castle explains why Lewes was built in that particular place. From there you can see how the Downs roll down to where the Ouse flows towards the sea at Newhaven and how the gap provides a natural gateway to the Weald. It stands to reason, therefore, that anyone commanding the heights at Lewes would also be in control of the Down trackways, the river crossing and the riverborne traffic as well. The castle might not look very tall when viewed from the High Street but the prospect from the top is wide-ranging and spectacular.

The nearer view of the jumble of different roofs and assorted chimney-pots which adorn the old houses is equally pleasing. It also shows how much has been preserved in Lewes. So often old photographs of a town provoke feelings of regret for how much has been lost, but Lewes has been fortunate in preserving its townscape so well. In fact it still conforms to Defoe's description as being 'well built and situated'. Let big brother Brighton continue on its brash way; Lewes will keep its select charm.

That is not to say that the good citizens of Lewes have ignored Brighton when it came to turning a honest penny. After all, Dr Richard Russell was a physician in Lewes before he moved his lucrative practice to Brighton in 1753. Then there was the famous discoverer of the iguanodon, Dr Gideon Mantell, who moved from Castle Place to Brighton in 1833.

But to go back to even earlier times, it was the Normans who really put Lewes on the map, although the place had also been important in Saxon times. William the Conqueror gave the Rape of Lewes to his favourite companion-in-arms, William de Warenne, who promptly set about building a magnificent castle to overawe the natives. Norman rule was an amalgam of military might and religion and William de Warenne and his mysterious wife Gundrada also created the important Priory of St Pancras. Gundrada's memorial stone, exquisitely carved in black marble, can still be seen today in the church of St John the Baptist, Southover. The carving looks so fresh it creates the illusion the Norman Conquest happened only yesterday.

It is a shame poor St Pancras has acquired such railway overtones and it is even more ironic that a railway line should pass right through the priory site. St Pancras himself was a lad of noble birth martyred at the age of fourteen, and a saint held in high regard in medieval times. It was to celebrate his feast day on 12 May 1264 that Henry III came to the Priory at Lewes, but the observance had an unexpected outcome for the Battle of Lewes was fought on 14 May. The king's army, although greatly outnumbering the barons', led by Simon de Montfort, lost the day. This victory is considered to be one of the foundation stones of parliamentary government.

It is interesting, when you reflect on the importance of the Priory, that Lewes should have evolved into a Protestant stronghold. The fact that in the 1550s seventeen Protestant martyrs were burned at the stake in the High Street remains fresh in the memory. Lewes has also chosen to remember 5 November each year in its own inimitable way – not to honour Guy Fawkes of course, but to celebrate the discovery of the Gunpowder Plot before Parliament could be blown up. During the Civil War Lewes was staunchly on the side of Parliament. In fact so warmly did the citizens view the campaign of Sir William Waller that they presented him with £50 as a mark of appreciation on his recapture of Arundel. At the Restoration Richard Cromwell made his escape to France by boarding a boat at Lewes.

By the eighteenth century Lewes had settled down to a prosperous existence, many houses were built, and important people took up residence. Well-to-do families living in the countryside found it convenient to own a town house in Lewes.

Naturally, not all the inhabitants belonged to the gentry and two anecdotes provide us with a glimpse of the harsher side of life. In September 1769 a dragoon was court-martialled at Lewes for desertion and sentenced to receive 500 lashes. He endured 300 lashes and the *Sussex Weekly Advertiser* happily concluded its report, 'the remaining 200 were forgiven him through the lenity [sic] of his colonel, who afterwards very humanely ordered him to be taken strict care of'.

Then there was the poor widow who in the 1840s used to earn her living by picking watercresses at Lewes and carrying them the 9 miles to Brighton to sell. Her little girl was decently dressed in a garment made of white rags sewn together and dyed purple with a pennyworth of logwood.

In 1806 the Act of 46 George III attempted to improve conditions in the town. People were requested to 'sweep or clean the foot-pavement before their houses at least once a week' or more often should the Commissioners request it. Failure to comply could result in a fine of up to 20s. Other regulations concerned the obstruction caused by signs or notices, and there was a rule that no new building could encroach beyond the old building line. Lastly, there was the injunction that a privy must only be emptied between 11.00 at night and 5.00 in the morning.

Lewes means many things to many people. To some a grim place of correction, as Lewes Prison (erected in the 1850s) was preceded by others including a Naval Prison. Then there is the solemn presence of the Law Courts, which have seen such celebrated trials as that of John George Haigh, the acid bath murderer. Nobody can forget that Lewes is important as an administrative centre since the great slab of County Hall is all too visible. But to others Lewes is synonymous with fun and fireworks, colourful costumes and huge bonfires on 5 November.

To the old time shepherds of the South Downs, Lewes meant the celebrated Sheep Fair which was held on 21 September every year. It was not only a time to sell sheep but also an opportunity to meet old friends at the Swan in the evening after the day's business was done. The shepherds called it Clothing Day too because they would call at Browne and Crosskey's shop in the High Street and climb the stairs to the clothing department, leaving their crooks and sheepdogs downstairs. The shop people obligingly put out packing cases on the pavement so that wives and friends could wait in comfort. A favourite purchase was a large white overcoat with a hand-stitched double seam. The coats were virtually waterproof and capable of protecting the shepherd in all weathers. However, at 32s. 6d. each they were expensive, and quite often the farmers would pay so that their employees could be properly clothed. Other items would include a smock in slate-grey or drab linen embellished with smocking, long tan leather gaiters and huge strong umbrellas covered in a green material which would soon weather to a bluish shade.

Lewes also had its thriving industries (and some remain). Milling, iron-founding and brewing were going on as well as all the work connected with the Ouse, such as small ship-building yards making barges for river work. It is difficult to believe but in March 1839 a seagoing brig of 61 tons called the *Lewes Castle* was launched from Rickman and Godlee's yard.

To the student of architecture Lewes provides a whole range of delights. Flint is much in evidence from the cobblestones in the centre of Keere Street to the fine knapped and squared flint used on some houses in the High Street. Flint was also used in the construction of all fourteen old churches, besides the castle, priory and prison. Mathematical tiles are unusual but at Lewes they have been hung on sixty buildings, while grey brick is another Lewes speciality. Nor must one forget the timber-framed buildings or the Caen stone of Southover Manor.

One of the strengths of Lewes is its continuity and Horsfield's description, penned in 1824, still holds good today: 'The town stands on the eastern declivity of one of those turf-covered eminences of the chalk formation, so well known and distinguished as the South Downs; and though its site is somewhat elevated, it is still surrounded on the south, east and west by an amphitheatre of bolder and loftier hills.'

SECTION ONE

Shops and Businesses

A SMILING DELIVERY LAD photographed in around 1907 with his horse and cart which advertises Ballard's Oat-Malt Stout. Ballard's were brewers as well as wine and spirit merchants and their premises were at High Street, Southover.

THE BUSY WORKSHOP of J.C.H. Martin's garage and repair premises in the High Street in around 1907.

COOMBS AND JEMPSON ran a cycle shop and a cycle repair business at 11 West Street, Lewes, and this photograph dates from around 1914. However, this shop was a short-lived enterprise because by 1918 the Coombs brothers had decided to concentrate on their Eastbourne shop.

A VIEW OF THE HIGH STREET taken in 1915. In the right foreground is a horse and cart belonging to Bourner, the carriers. Two or three times a week, one of Bourner's carts would start from the Swan in Southover High Street for destinations such as Brighton, Framfield, Hadlow Down, Brightling, Hurst Green, Isfield, Maresfield and Uckfield.

THE ENTRANCE TO THE PHOENIX IRON WORKS in around 1903. Alderman Every, owner and manager, was very interested in the old iron-founding days of Sussex and he created his own museum at the works where he displayed his collection which included 100 firebacks.

A BUSY SCENE IN AROUND 1903 inside the foundry at the Phoenix Iron Works. The foundry measured 150 ft by 138 ft. The management were model employers and provided their workforce with many facilities not usually offered to the working man at that date.

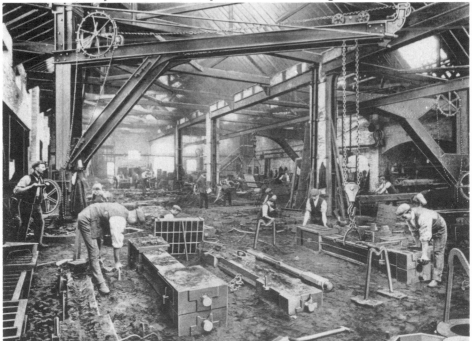

ANOTHER VIEW OF THE INTERIOR of the Phoenix Iron Works. The men appear to be hard at work on cast-iron columns.

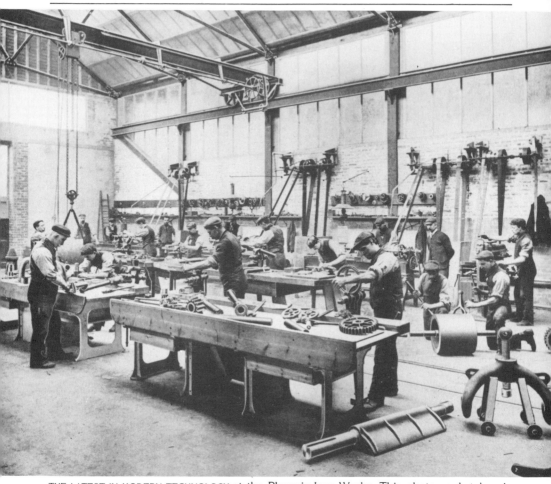

THE LATEST IN MODERN TECHNOLOGY at the Phoenix Iron Works. This photograph taken in around 1903 shows a corner of the new fitting shop which measured 60 ft by 27 ft.

THIS SUMPTUOUS PIECE OF IRONWORK was featured in the Phoenix Catalogue of 1903. It was in fact the cricket pavilion in Lord Sheffield's park.

THE LOADING-UP YARD at the Phoenix Iron Works. On the side of the carts can be seen 'J.Every'. The Everys ran the works for three generations. The business was founded in 1832 and closed in 1951.

AN OLD PRINT showing Harvey's Brewery, founded in 1790 and still going strong today. The view remains substantially the same although the building behind the tall chimney has gone. The premises were rebuilt in 1880.

A WINTER SCENE at Harvey's Brewery dating from the 1870s. Note the two sheds in front of the chimney which do not appear in the previous photograph. The heavily laden barge is called the *Centaur*.

A GROUP OF WORKERS stare fixedly at the camera while those in charge seat themselves on small barrels. The photograph dates from the 1870s and the variety of headgear is interesting.

A REFLECTIVE TIME at Harvey's Brewery. Workers contemplate the scene when the Ouse burst its banks. The photograph probably dates from around 1911.

ST ANNE'S HILL photographed in around 1904. On the right is the shop of John William Bennett, hairdresser and tobacconist. He also had shops in Cliffe High Street and Station Street.

THE PELHAM GARAGE was in the High Street near the Pelham Arms. The photograph was taken in around 1924 and the proprietor was W.E. Witcher. Any make of new car could be supplied and Mr Witcher was also prepared to give advice on the purchase of secondhand cars.

CARVILLS WAS A FIRM with diverse interests. As well as removals and storage, they traded as cabinet makers, upholsterers and bedding manufacturers. Their premises were at 24 High Street (next door to the Cinema de Luxe) and at 34 and 35 Friars Walk (near All Saints'). The photograph dates from around 1924.

J. BLACKETT & SON,

Oil, Colour & Italian Warehousemen.

Patent Medicines and Proprietary Articles.

———

Household Requisites, Brooms, Brushes, etc.

Lamps & Glasses in great variety.

———

Builders and Painters supp'ied with White Lead, Colours, Varnishes, and Gold Leaf, at Lowest Prices.

———

Paint of all Colours carefully Prepared.

SCHOOL HILL, HIGH STREET, LEWES.

THIS INTERESTING ADVERTISEMENT for J. Blackett and Son appeared in Pike's Lewes Directory of 1905.

SECTION TWO

Western Road and High Street

THE WELL-KNOWN FAÇADE of Shelley's Hotel photographed before it became a hotel and just after it had been used as a hospital for officers during the First World War.

21

A SUNNY DAY BUT A MUDDY WESTERN ROAD photographed in around 1915. Note the little dog so obviously unconcerned about trotting along the public highway.

AN OLD VIEW OF LEWES which makes the main street look like a cloistered cathedral close. Note also the preponderance of ivy.

A DESERTED HIGH STREET (from the traffic point of view) looking towards Rotten Row in around 1921.

THIS VIEW DATES FROM AROUND 1906. Behind the man pushing the handcart is a butcher's shop at 97 High Street belonging to Alfred Appleby, and next door is the business of R. Barber, practical bookbinders.

THE CLOCK BY ST MICHAEL'S CHURCH is a prominent feature of this scene photographed in around 1905. The young couple have just passed the Brewers Inn kept by Horace William Graham.

THIS PHOTOGRAPH WAS TAKEN looking the opposite way to the previous one and dates from around 1922. The County Garage and Engineering Works on the right at 170 High Street are run by J.S. Richardson. The car's registration number is LA 3864.

UNLIKE MANY OLD STREET SCENES, this view taken in around 1904 makes the road look quite crowded. On the right at 70 High Street is the shop of Frederick Pryor, pork butcher.

THE UNMISTAKABLE SHAPE of the White Hart Hotel dominates this view of the High Street taken in around 1904. Next door is the little Unicorn Inn with its swinging shield-like sign.

LOOKING WEST ALONG THE HIGH STREET in around 1911. On the left Boots cash chemist are at Nos. 51 and 52, and on the right are the Crown Courts dating from 1812 and beyond them the YMCA occupies No. 183.

WHEN THIS PHOTGRAPH WAS TAKEN in around 1890 Mrs Margaret Hardy ran the tobacconist's shop at 49 High Street. Note the shop on the left selling straw boaters for summer wear and the fine gas lamp-standard in front.

THE HIGH STREET in around 1915 showing Ye Olde Tobacco Shoppe at No. 49 run by Hubert Woolmore and behind it at Nos. 47 and 48 are the Dining Rooms run by C.H. Longhurst Marsh.

A BUSTLING SCENE OUTSIDE THE TOWN HALL in around 1903. It was then a new building, having been erected in 1893. Note the hanging lamp above the entrance with its ornate bracket.

A STUDY OF THE TOWN HALL by Francis Frith in around 1903. Nearby Charles Morrish advertises his business, described in Pike's Directory as 'linen draper, silk mercers, ladies' outfitters, dress and mantle makers'.

High Street, Lewes, Top of School Hill.

THE TOP OF SCHOOL HILL in 1906 showing the magnificent three-branched lamp-standard on the site now occupied by the war memorial. On the left at 192 High Street Mrs Eliza Addison ran her stationer's business while upstairs R. Elgar Deuchar followed the trade of 'artificial teeth maker'.

THE WAR MEMORIAL with its fine bronze figures was erected in 1922. This photograph was taken on a misty morning in the 1930s and the Portland stone already shows signs of weathering.

THIS BEAUTIFULLY CLEAR PHOTOGRAPH OF SCHOOL HILL was taken by Francis Frith in 1894. Nelson's Household Helps occupies 194 High Street and the board above the shop advertises 'Bassinettes [*sic*], Mail Carts, Wringers and Sewing Machines'.

A MISTY WINTER'S MORNING ON SCHOOL HILL in the 1890s. The tower of Harvey's Brewery is silhouetted in the background. A close-up of the shop on the left, which sold paint and household items, can be seen on p. 20.

SCHOOL HILL IN AROUND 1922. Note that Nelson's have expanded their range of wares while Milward's have just started up at 197 High Street.

A TRANQUIL VIEW dating from the 1920s with a solitary motor car cruising sedately down the middle of the road. On the right a sign advertises the Cinema de Luxe.

LOOKING UP SCHOOL HILL in the 1920s with the Cinema de Luxe in the left foreground. The current film is only modestly advertised on the pillars.

Twittens and Streets

A PARTICULARLY FINE AND UNUSUAL VIEW of Grange Road taken in around 1906.

A CHARMING VIEW OF POTTER'S LANE in around 1909, an old corner of Lewes. The grand houses of Grange Road are seen looming on the horizon.

MARIE FROST AND HER BROTHER JOFFRE (named after the French general in the First World War) stand outside their house at 20 Leicester Road in 1922.

THE TOP OF KEERE STREET in around 1906. Henry Pinyoun kept a bakery at No. 1 for many years. Further down at No. 10 there was a beer shop run by Harry Winder.

View from Keere Street   Lewes.

THE BOTTOM OF KEERE STREET photographed in around 1909 with two rather sedate young ladies wearing enormous flat caps. A corner of Southover Grange can be seen in the background.

THERE ARE SO MANY VENERABLE BUILDINGS in Lewes that you might think this is another one. In fact the Council Offices were built in 1913 in best mock-Tudor style. The postcard dates from around 1930.

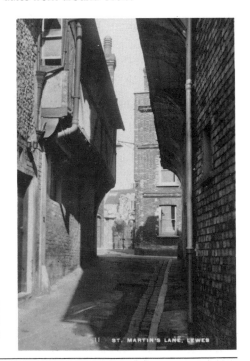

THE NORTH END OF ST MARTIN'S LANE in around 1930. It is interesting to note that in 1622 John Rowe said that it was also known as Snelling's Lane.

MRS ELIZABETH HIDE photographed with her children outside her house at 5 St Martin's Lane in around 1920. Back row, left to right, Mary and Percy; front row, Kathleen, Joan and 'Bud'.

THIS PHOTOGRAPH OF THE AVENUE was taken by Francis Frith. When the Avenue was constructed in 1907 it was called D'Albiac Avenue. But this proved too much of a mouthful for the residents and it was altered at their request in 1908.

A QUIET CORNER OF PRIORY CRESCENT with the castle just visible in the background. The original postcard was coloured and dates from around 1912.

THE STEEP INCLINE OF CHAPEL HILL photographed in around 1906. It was once called East Street and marks the site of an ancient route up over the Downs to Glynde.

BULL HOUSE photographed in the 1920s. Thomas Paine, author of *The Rights of Man*, arrived here in 1768. It is fitting that the board on the right of the picture proclaims the house to be the meeting place of the Lewes Liberal and Radical Party. The house was restored by Alderman J.H. Every in 1922.

STATION STREET WAS ONCE CALLED ST MARY'S LANE after a church which used to stand at the High Street end. On the right can be seen the Methodist Church which was built in 1867. It was closed in 1973. The postcard dates from around 1915.

SECTION FOUR

Panoramas

A WONDERFULLY ATMOSPHERIC PHOTOGRAPH of Lewes from Malling Hill taken by F. Douglas Miller in around 1905.

LOOKING DOWN ON THE TOWN FROM THE COOMBE in 1905.

A VIEW LOOKING TOWARDS LEWES along the Miller's Walk taken in around 1936.

SCUDDING CLOUDS have been skilfully painted on to this old view of Lewes. The shop in the foreground advertises its services as a furniture dealer and coal merchant.

Aeroplane view of Lewes, showing Avenue and Battlefield
(Battle fought between Simon de Montfort and Henry III in 1264)

A NOVELTY VIEW OF LEWES taken from an aeroplane. The stately houses of the Avenue are seen across the Paddock.

A VIEW OF LEWES which sums up one of its charms – the frequent glimpses of the Downs. The photograph dates from the 1920s and the church in the background is St Thomas's.

A LOOK AT LEWES FROM THE GOLF LINKS in around 1908. Note the gas holders prominent in the foreground which indicate the industrial importance of the River Ouse in former times.

Castle and Priory

A BEAUTIFULLY CLEAR STUDY OF THE BARBICAN in which the stones could almost be counted. Castlegate House peeps over the wall. The card was specially produced by Boots the Chemists.

33860 LEWES: THE BARBICAN, W.

AN OLD VIEW OF THE BARBICAN which includes a liveried coachman to add a touch of elegance.

Lewes Castle

A MOST ROMANTIC VIEW OF LEWES, all ruins and ivy with not too many houses visible. This postcard was sent in 1907.

A STUDY OF LEWES CASTLE BY FRANCIS FRITH in around 1903. It shows the keep looking west. The large doorway is not part of the original structure, having been inserted in the nineteenth century.

A VIEW ACROSS THE GUN GARDEN towards the keep taken in around 1910.

IT IS ALWAYS INTERESTING to look down on Lewes from the castle. Note the profusion of chimney stacks and the telegraph poles.

THE RUINS OF THE GREAT PRIORY OF ST PANCRAS photographed in around 1900. It is remarkable that portions of the building still stand 400 years after Thomas Cromwell engaged an Italian engineer to destroy them.

ANOTHER VIEW OF THE PRIORY RUINS. In its heyday the Priory church was 450 ft in length.

Cliffe, Malling and Southover

ON THE RIGHT OF CLIFFE BRIDGE stands the Bear Hotel. This view was taken in around 1906 when Miss Julia David ran the Bear Hotel and the Lewes Cyclists' Club had their headquarters there. The hotel was destroyed by fire in 1918.

THE PROMINENT SHOP in this photograph of Cliffe High Street taken in around 1906 is the Rice Brothers' premises. They were saddlers and there are some farrier's leather aprons hanging by the door. The Rices had another shop at Haywards Heath.

A BRIGHT SUMMER'S DAY IN CLIFFE HIGH STREET in around 1912. The butchers, W. and R. Fletcher, are at No. 9 and further on a giant pair of spectacles can be seen acting as a shop sign.

CLIFFE HIGH STREET in around 1906. The London and Provincial Meat Store can be seen on the left at No. 22 with posters advertising their Christmas Club. The sign near the drawn down blind reads 'Good accommodation for cyclists'.

CLIFFE HIGH ST. LEWES. 4.

FURTHER ALONG CLIFFE HIGH STREET. The long barber's pole appears to be suspended from the St Thomas's tower.

FRANCIS FRITH TOOK THIS PHOTOGRAPH of Cliffe High Street in around 1903. The viewpoint is at the opposite end of the street from the previous photograph. On the right a hoarding advertises George Bates and Sons as 'Metalworks, Plumber, Painter, Glazier, Home Decorator'.

DOWNS, FROM CLIFF HILL, LEWES.
71754

THE MARTYRS' MEMORIAL was unveiled on Cliffe Hill on 8 May 1901. It is a suitably sombre obelisk commemorating as it does the seventeen Protestant martyrs burned to death in the High Street in the 1550s.

A CLEAR VIEW OF MALLING STREET looking towards Malling Hill photographed in around 1905 by F. Douglas Miller.

ALTHOUGH THE VIEWPOINT of this photograph is almost the same as the previous one, it was taken some years later. Note how the little shop on the right now dominates its neighbours with its additional storey and how ivy has covered the large white house. In the background are the Wheatsheaf Inn and Elmsley's Brewery.

THIS THIRD PHOTOGRAPH OF MALLING STREET dates from 1904 and gives a clearer view of the brewery building and the houses on the other side of the street.

AN ATMOSPHERIC STUDY OF SOUTHOVER GRANGE in around 1904. The house was built in 1572 of Caen stone which was conveniently at hand from the dismantled Priory.

LEWES AND ITS CASTLE PHOTOGRAPHED in around 1906. This view emphasizes the way the town has grown up on different levels.

FORTUNATELY THIS VIEW OF ANN OF CLEVES HOUSE has not altered much since it was photographed in around 1906 but the muddy road gives a clue to its early date.

SECTION SEVEN

Road and Rail

TWO DETERMINED LOOKING WOMEN are keeping an eye on the toll-gate at Southerham in this photograph probably dating from the 1870s. Their small cottage has a very tall chimney.

THIS PHOTOGRAPH OF THE OLD TOLL-HOUSE at Ashcombe was taken in around 1910 when it still had a ragged thatched roof. The structure itself was built in around 1810.

LEWES RAILWAY STATION photographed in June 1888.

THIS INTERESTING OLD PHOTOGRAPH shows part of the former Lewes railway station. It was situated in Friars Walk, but in 1857 the new station was opened.

THE HORSE-CABS WAIT PATIENTLY for the next train to arrive in 1909. It must be winter because the horses are wearing blankets and the cabs have their hoods drawn up.

AN IMPRESSIVE VIEW OF LEWES RAILWAY STATION in around 1903 showing the cast-iron columns manufactured at John Every's Phoenix Iron Works. On the left there are two advertisements for the Great Western Railway featuring train times from Paddington to Birmingham, and Paddington to South Wales.

ANOTHER VIEW OF THE STATION with some more examples from the Phoenix Iron Works. Compare the more massive columns with the slender ones of the previous photograph.

A VIEW OF THE CASTLE as seen from the railway station and on the right an example of how a horse and cab were turned out in the summer. The original postcard was coloured.

Police and Fire Brigade

LEWES POLICE photographed in 1879 by J. Frisby. Police Constable 118 Samuel Barnard is seated second from the left. It is notable that out of twenty-two men, only three are clean shaven.

AN INTERESTING PHOTOGRAPH which demonstrates that being on point duty was once an almost leisurely affair. On the right a sale is taking place in Horace W. Moore's shop at 1 Malling Street, general draper and ladies' outfitter. The date is around 1934.

THE LEWES VOLUNTEER FIRE BRIGADE photographed in the 1870s when Captain Duplock was in charge.

OUTSIDE THE NEWLY-BUILT FIRE STATION the men of the Lewes Fire Brigade pose proudly aboard their horse-drawn manual fire-engine in 1907.

THE LATEST IN FIRE-FIGHTING EQUIPMENT AT LEWES — a steamer — on display in 1907. The straw-hatted man in the left foreground points the nozzle straight at the camera.

THE LEWES FIRE BRIGADE photographed in 1909. Charles Hide stands on the extreme left.

SECTION NINE

People

A CRICKET TEAM photographed on 10 July 1882 at the Dripping Pan.

A FINE BODY OF MEN: the Sussex Artillery Militia in around 1880 photographed in the grounds of Saxonbury, a large house on the Kingston road. Their mascot obviously could not keep still.

AN IMPOSING GROUP OF WORTHIES, including the Marquess of Abergavenny and William Langham Christie, MP for Lewes, photographed in 1881 in front of the race stand at the Conservative Fête.

ROBERT ALBERT STOCK FRCVS poses with his model patient, known as Railway Jack, standing perkily on his three legs. Stock lived for many years at Radstock House, Cliffe High Street. Railway Jack used to enjoy travelling the railways on his own and visiting his many friends and admirers. In 1887 it was even stated that he had been patted on the head by the Prince of Wales at Ascot.

CHARLES AND ELIZABETH HIDE pose in the back garden of 5 St Martin's Lane with their children in around 1902. The children are, left to right, Bill, Fred, Lizzie, Chris and Dick. On the left can be seen the wire mesh of the chicken run belonging to their next door neighbour Mr Cole, while to the right the family's tin bath peeps from behind the rigged-up background.

DR LEONARD HEDLEY BURROWS was vicar of Hove and bishop of Lewes from 1909 until 1914 after which he became bishop of Sheffield. Note the wide collar, the buttoned clerical gaiters and the delightful-looking mongrel at Mrs Burrows' feet.

THE LEWES BOROUGH BONFIRE SOCIETY photographed in 1921. Back row: second from left, Fred Hendy (one time licensee of the Bell Inn, Eastport Lane), third from left, Mrs Piper, sixth from left, Fred Wadey. Third row: second from left, Steve Holder (a butcher in Priory Street for many years), third from right, Mr Palmer. Second row: first left, 'Arty' Cox (a postman for many years), fifth from left, 'Min' Puttock, second from right, Fred Hide. Front row: fifth from left, George Parsons, third from right, Lizzie Holder, second from right, Nan Mcdonough, first right, Elizabeth Hide.

A HAPPY FAMILY GROUP taken in 1922 when Fred Hide married Nan Mcdonough.

THE WEDDING of Kathleen Hide and John Kettle in 1938. Kathleen was the youngest of seventeen children and there was about a year's difference in age between her and her neice Betty Holder who married Harry Kettle, the bridegroom's brother. Harry Kettle was killed in Burma during the war. The photograph was taken at the back of the White Hart.

YOUNG FRED HIDE POSES PROUDLY in the uniform of the Royal Sussex Regiment in around 1915.

A SMARTLY TURNED OUT PERCY HIDE photographed outside 30 Paddock Road in around 1932. At the time he was under butler to Lady Buxton. Later he became valet to Sir Anthony Eden.

TWO SISTERS DRESSED UP for the Borough Bonfire Society in around 1932 are Lizzie Holder and Maggie Parsons.

GEORGE PARSONS dressed up for the St Anne's Bonfire Society in around 1935.

A HAPPY GROUP ON A PUB OUTING in 1934. The pub in question was the Bell Inn, Eastport Lane (now gone) and the landlord Fred Hendy stands in the centre of the back row dressed in a light-coloured jacket and hat. Directly in front of him his wife Min is wearing a black hat. Kathleen Hide sits on the extreme right of the front row.

'BUD' HIDE walking past the Town Hall in around 1936.

A DELIGHTFUL STUDY OF LANDPORT, near Lewes, in around 1908. It would be interesting to know if the smartly-dressed man was the father of all the children.

MRS ELIZABETH HIDE posing as a bathing beauty in around 1936 in the back garden of 5 St Martin's Lane. The white dots in her costume are moth holes!

SECTION TEN

Schools

PELL'S SCHOOL IN AROUND 1927. Back row: third from left, John Parsons, fifth from left, Denis Eede. Second row: first left, Frank Newnham, third from left, Gander, fifth from left, Woolard (his father was a lamplighter with the nickname of 'Slippery'), sixth from left, Arnold. Third row, third from right, Peggy Tyrrell. Front row, third from left, Denis Smith, first right, Frank Martin ('Snaggy').

PELLS BOYS' SCHOOL ATHLETIC TEAM OF 1928 (winner of the Senior and Junior 'Victor Ludorum' trophies). The Headmaster Harry Bradford stands on the left.

ST PANCRAS SCHOOL CELEBRATES EMPIRE DAY in 1921 at Ham Lane. Among the children in the front row are Leslie Gale, James Harper, Joffre Frost, Ronald Rainbird and Dora Piper.

THE INFANTS' CLASS OF ST PANCRAS SCHOOL in 1925. Back row, left to right: Ronnie Whitehorn, Margery Burns, Jack Chestney, Bert Downey. Second row: Ted Richardson, Patrick Crock, Tony Taylor, Bert Cornford, C. Penfold, -?-, Walter Dunk, Vera Heasman. Third row: Marie Frost, Blanch Breeds, Patricia Lucas, Margaret Peacock, E. Chapman, -?-, Patricia Cox, Joan Dean. Front row: Joseph Cramer, -?-, Fred Goldsmith, -?-, Tony Treadaway, Bobby Bernard.

THE CHILDREN OF ST PANCRAS DRESS UP for the May Day Revels but the birds look remarkably sinister.

THE CENTRAL SCHOOL SPORTS TEAM in 1931. Back row, left to right, Pearl Rawles, Gwendoline Williams, Sylvia Baker, Ivy Brooks, Joyce Buckwell, Peggy Skinner, Ruby Dawes, Emily Stevens, Edith Pollard. Front row, Doris Wicks, -?-, Judy Roser, Doris Denman, Kathleen Hide, Dora Carter, Enid Tucker, Kathleen Sargeant.

A CLOSE-UP OF THE OLD GRAMMAR SCHOOL at the turn of the century when its fine knapped flintwork was completely obscured by ivy.

THE CRICKET TEAM FIELDED BY THE OLD GRAMMAR SCHOOL in the 1920s. Back row, left to right, Mr Williams, B.W. James, B.B. Brook, H.R. Savage, T.G. Skipworth, H.A. George, A.D. Catt, H. Wilson, Mr Fretwell. Front row, P.R. Parkhurst, E.G. Skipworth, F. Powell, D. Stewart.

THE GRAMMAR SCHOOL, LEWES, SUSSEX,

OCTOBER,  1924.

THE STAFF AND PUPILS OF THE OLD GRAMMAR SCHOOL photographed in October 1924. The smiling clerical gentleman in the centre is the Headmaster, the Revd E. Griffiths.

WHEN THE OLD GRAMMAR SCHOOL WAS PHOTOGRAPHED in 1924, the result was one of those popular panoramic shots. This photograph represents the right wing. The school cap leaves much to be desired. Note how almost every boy in the back row appears to be wearing a cap of the wrong size.

MORE PUPILS FROM THE 1924 PHOTOGRAPH of the Old Grammar School. It seems that the few girls who attended were not obliged to wear a uniform.

LEICESTER HOUSE SCHOOL in 1951 when the principal was E. Hoffman. The school was at 7 King Henry's Road.

SECTION ELEVEN

Events

A SMART TURN-OUT FOR THE JUDGES' ESCORT at Lewes Assizes in 1878. It is to be hoped that the muddy state of the road did not ruin the effect.

THE FIRE on 4 October 1904 completely destroyed Mr F.H. Dusart's premises. He ran two shops and was a hairdresser, tobacconist and fancy dealer. Mr Dusart had to jump from a third-storey window and he was closely followed by his two sons, aged thirteen and ten. Mrs Dusart, a younger child and a maid were rescued by ladder.

THE AFTERMATH OF THE GREAT FIRE of 4 October 1904. It was claimed that if it had not been for the assistance of the up-to-date steamer fire-engine from Brighton, all of the property up to Bull Lane might have been destroyed.

ne Bridge after the fire at Lewes 18. 6

AN EVEN LARGER FIRE OCCURRED on 18 June 1918. The Bear Hotel was completely gutted; Strickland's granary and Stevenson's granary were destroyed as well as the bridge between the two. But it is good to know that a sitting hen and eight terrified horses were rescued safely.

THE SUSSEX YEOMANRY CAVALRY were formed in 1901 and this photograph shows them at their ablutions in camp near Lewes in 1905.

THE SUSSEX YEOMANRY CAVALRY line up for inspection in 1905. The cavalry mantles or greatcoats were of voluminous proportions so that, when mounted, the material would cover the horse's hindquarters. The uniform also included a slouch hat adorned with a bright blue emu feather plume.

UNDER CANVAS NEAR LEWES YET AGAIN. This photograph was published by the local firm of A.M. Bliss. The horse looks somewhat truncated with his close-cropped tail.

H.R.H. PRINCESS HENRY OF BATTENBERG
OPENS NEW LEWES HOSPITAL
PPCo 2.   FEB. 2nd 1910.

IT WAS SUCH A MISERABLE RAINY DAY when Princess Henry of Battenberg opened Lewes Hospital on 2 February 1910 that the guard of honour had to turn up the collars of their greatcoats. The princess was Queen Victoria's youngest daughter.

THE FLOODS AT SOUTHOVER IN 1916.

A COLOURFUL PROCESSION TO CELEBRATE EMPIRE DAY at Lewes in 1911. The photograph was something of a disappointment to Aunt Lily (who sent the postcard) because the little girls in bonnets dressed as milkmaids were no doubt very fetching but she could not make out which one was Queenie.

THIS IS HOW ST GEORGE'S DAY WAS CELEBRATED at Lewes in the 1920s.

THE INHABITANTS OF LEICESTER ROAD celebrate VE Day in 1945.

Parks

THE STILL WATER OF THE PELLS looking towards St John sub Castro captured by F. Douglas Miller in around 1905.

THE ORIGINAL POSTCARD is coloured and the lady wears a pink gown. It is pleasant to reflect that there used to be a swannery around here owned by the Prior of Lewes.

A RATHER FADED PHOTOGRAPH OF THE PELLS but note the disdainful expression on the faces of the girls as they look at the boys fooling around.

SNOW SCENE, THE PELLS, LEWES.

THIS VIEW OF THE PELLS is taken from the same point as the previous one (note the circular seat around the tree) but after a snowfall. The postcard was sent from the Chaplain's House at Lewes Prison in February 1909.

A WINTRY-LOOKING RECREATION GROUND, but while one little girl wears a pinafore the other is so solidly dressed movement must have been restricted.

SECTION THIRTEEN

Farming

AN OX DRIVER with his characteristic long goad of hazel looks reflectively at his cart full of turnips at a farm near Lewes in 1906.

THIS PHOTOGRAPH was taken by S.G. Jupp on the Downs near Falmer in around 1905. The ox team consists of eight Welsh runts and each pair is coupled with a wooden yoke.

A TEAM OF SIX OXEN photographed in around 1907 at Howesdean near Newmarket Hill. The oxen are wearing horn caps to prevent them from injuring each other and next around their mouths to stop them from grazing.

SHEPHERD WOOLER with his trusted dog by the sheep-fold on Mount Caburn. His crook was made at Pyecombe Forge.

THIS VIEW SHOWS SOME FINE SHEEP up for sale in September 1923, with the light reflecting from their fleeces and every man's head with a hat on it.

THE SCENE AT LEWES SHEEP FAIR on 21 September 1923. Note the sheep-dog hard at work in the foreground.

SECTION FOURTEEN

Windmills

THE YARD OF SAMUEL MEDHURST AND SON, millwrights and engineers, at St Anne's, 17 and 18 High Street in 1879. Samuel Medhurst sports a white beard and his wife Philadelphia stands at the front door. It is a sad fact that this couple lost many of their children in infancy. Between 1828 and 1846 Samuel, Philadelphia, Benjamin, Naomi, Reuben and Frank all died at a few months; Naomi died at three years old.

MALLING MILL photographed on a wonderfully crisp day in around 1905 by F. Douglas Miller. It was the scene of several accidents, the worst occurring in January 1817 before the mill was heightened. A woman called Wood tried to take a short cut with the result that she was hit by two of the sweeps, fracturing her arm, collar-bone and thigh. She died shortly afterwards. The mill was burnt down on 8 September 1908.

LOOKING DOWN ON MALLING HIGH STREET in around 1905. In the background can be seen the white sweeps of Malling Mill, attributed to Samuel Medhurst.

ANOTHER PHOTOGRAPH BY F. DOUGLAS MILLER, taken from Rotten Row in around 1905. On the horizon can be seen two windmills popularly known as the Kingston Mills. On the left is the stump of a white smock-mill called Old Duck because it used to roll while at work – it fell down in a storm in 1891. The other one is a white post-mill, also called the Southern Mill, which was pulled down with ropes in August 1913.

ASHCOMBE MILL was known affectionately as Old Six Sweeps. It was a unique mill and very much a Lewes creation because it was built by the Medhurst firm and the windshaft was cast by the Phoenix Iron Works.

THIS MILL was known variously as the Town Mill and the Gaol Mill but at the time this photograph was taken (around 1870) it was called Shelley's Mill after the miller Joseph Shelley who worked it. It is interesting to note that the mill had to be raised after the prison was built in the 1850s because the structure was blocking off the wind.

River Ouse

AN INTERESTING VIEW taken by F. Douglas Miller in around 1905 of the chalk pits at Southerham. The layers of hewn chalk can be clearly seen.

THE OUSE portrayed as an industrial highway in around 1912. The board on the right advertises the Lewes Portland Cement and Lime Company.

THIS STUDY OF THE CHALK CLIFFS AT LEWES was taken by Francis Frith. Note the two tall chimneys reflected in the water.

A VENERABLE PHOTOGRAPH OF THE OUSE near Lewes. It is appropriate to recall that in the 1870s barges used to come up the river from Newhaven to sell fresh fish to the Lewes townspeople and that the town crier would shout the information 'Sixteen mackerel for 1s. or scallops for tuppence a dozen'.

AN IDYLLIC VIEW OF THE OUSE in around 1905. The three lads, two of them sporting Eton collars, add a spot of local colour.

A TRANQUIL STUDY OF THE OUSE approaching Lewes taken by F. Douglas Miller in around 1908.

SECTION SIXTEEN

Churches

ST JOHN SUB CASTRO was built in 1839 and the battlemented towers must have been inspired by the castle. This photograph dates from around 1908. The lady pushing the pram has had a steep climb up St John's Hill.

ST ANNE'S CHURCH photographed in around 1908. On the west side of the churchyard there are many memorials to the Medhurst family, a photograph of whom appears on p.125.

AN OLD VIEW OF THE INTERIOR OF ST ANNE'S CHURCH showing the splendid basket-work relief on the twelfth-century font.

THIS WAS HOW THE HIGH ALTAR OF ST MICHAEL'S appeared in around 1916. Note the six candlesticks – St Michael's was an early adherent to the High Church movement, a fact which caused much indignation in several parishioners in 1851.

SOME VIEWS OF LEWES DO NOT ALTER MUCH over the years – this is St Michael's in around 1912. The postcard is interesting because it is embossed with 'The Grammar School, Lewes' (presumably for pupils to send home) and this one is inscribed with '*un bon baiser*' and was sent to an address in Dieppe.

A STUDY OF THE CHURCH OF ST JOHN THE BAPTIST, by Francis Frith. The church is famous for the beautiful grave-slab made for Gundrada who died in 1085.

THE INTERIOR OF ST JOHN THE BAPTIST photographed in around 1906 with a close-up of the ornate chandelier and curiously enough no cross or flowers on the altar.

A VIEW OF ALL SAINTS' CHURCH in around 1906 with the tower heavily mantled with ivy. The imposing churchyard memorials are an indication of the many worthy citizens buried here.

THE STATELY INTERIOR OF ST THOMAS'S photographed in around 1906, apparently much in need of some restoration work on the walls. The church is well endowed with royal coats of arms; there are Elizabeth I's painted on plaster, and George I's painted on wood.

THE IVY-CLAD TOWER OF ST THOMAS'S pictured in around 1906. The church's full title is St Thomas à Becket-in-the-Cliffe and it is supposed to be on the site of a religious house dedicated to the memory of the recently martyred Archbishop of Canterbury, 'this turbulent priest', who was murdered inside his own cathedral in 1170.

THE CHURCH OF ST MICHAEL THE ARCHANGEL at Malling photographed by F. Douglas Miller in around 1905. There is an interesting literary connection because the diarist John Evelyn, writing in the year 1627, mentions the church being consecrated and states that he 'layd one of the first stones'.

THE SOMEWHAT AUSTERE INTERIOR OF ST MICHAEL'S, Malling, photographed by C.V. Travers of Hove. When the church was brand new, a vicar's daughter called Anne Sadler came here to be married in 1636. Her bridegroom was John Harvard, founder of Harvard University in Cambridge, Massachusetts, America's oldest university.

THE INTERIOR of the Roman Catholic Church of St Pancras photographed in around 1908. The occasion must have been a major festival because every spare inch is covered either by flowers or candles.

SECTION SEVENTEEN

Interiors

A NOSTALGIC LOOK AT THE WINTER GARDEN at the White Hart Hotel in around 1905 when Henry Tuff was the proprietor.

AN INTERESTING OLD PHOTOGRAPH showing an interior of one of the rooms in Anne of Cleves House as it looked in around 1910.

THIS IS HOW THE INSIDE OF THE LAMB APPEARED in the 1930s. Note the preponderance of Lloyd Loom furniture – both chairs and tables. It is interesting to reflect that the wheel of fashion has come full circle and such pieces would be much sought after today.

AN OLD POSTCARD of the interior of the Town Hall showing the magnificent Elizabethan staircase brought from Slaugham Place by Thomas Sergison in the 1730s to adorn the Star Inn at Lewes.

Kingston

THIS PHOTOGRAPH, taken in around 1905, makes Kingston look as though it was miles away from anywhere. In fact Kingston is only two and a half miles south-west of Lewes.

A BRIGHT SUMMER'S AFTERNOON IN KINGSTON in around 1905. Note the thatched roof of the cottage on the left.

ALTHOUGH THIS PHOTOGRAPH and the one above were both taken by F. Douglas Miller, it is clear that several years separate them. The thatched roof has gone and the near cottage has been painted and the garden planted up. There is also a difference in the height of the fir trees further along the road.

IT IS FITTING that Kingston's church is dedicated to St Pancras because the great Cluniac Priory at Lewes had the same dedication.

THIS LARGE IMPOSING HOUSE stands opposite the church at Kingston. This view dates from around 1912.

THIS VIEW of around 1905 emphasizes how close Kingston is to the Downs and one almost expects a shepherd and flock to come round the corner.

A NOSTALGIC LOOK AT OLD FARMING METHODS. F. Douglas Miller took this study on the hills near Kingston in around 1905.

Glynde

THIS DELIGHTFUL PHOTOGRAPH OF GLYNDE dates from around 1908. Note the interesting bicycle and side-car arrangement and the hanging sign outside the shop advertising Nectar tea.

IN THIS PHOTOGRAPH taken in around 1906, it looks as though news of the photographer's arrival has brought all the young people into the street.

GLYNDE CHURCH AND LICH-GATE photographed in around 1908. The church was built in the 1760s and paid for entirely by Dr Trevor, Bishop of Durham.

THE LITTLE BOY in the Huckleberry-style hat stands in front of the New Forge in around 1908. The building was famous for its giant horseshoe.

Glynde, Sussex.

ANOTHER VIEW OF TRANQUIL GLYNDE in around 1906. Note how two traditional Sussex building materials are represented here – flint built cottages on the left and weather boarding above the shop on the right.

EVERYBODY'S IDEA of how a peaceful Sussex village used to look. However, the smoking chimney suggests at least one housewife has been busy baking.

A FLOCK OF SHEEP PASSING THROUGH GLYNDE over the railway bridge is an appropriate sight since it was at Glynde that John Ellman perfected the famous breed of Southdown sheep.

SECTION TWENTY

Ringmer

F. DOUGLAS MILLER took a series of photographs of Ringmer in around 1905 and children are to be found in all of them. In this one two little girls pose in front of Springate Cottages.

A HORSE-DRAWN DELIVERY VAN plods slowly past the Green while the children crowd round the Ringmer village pump erected in 1883.

THE ANCHOR INN AT RINGMER photographed in around 1905 when John Skinner was the landlord. The Anchor seems an unlikely name for an inland village pub but there was also an Old Ship.

A FINE VIEW OF ST MARY, RINGMER, with the children standing decorously in the background. It is worth recalling that in the bad old days when Sussex roads were notorious quagmires, it took eight oxen to pull Sir Herbert Springett in his carriage to this church.

THIS COLOURED POSTCARD, depicting a different view of Springate Cottages, was produced in around 1906.

THE VILLAGE OF RINGMER not only had its own Green and pump but boasted its own Parish Room. This postcard was also brightly coloured.

Southease, Rodmell and Offham

A DELIGHTFUL STUDY by F. Douglas Miller of Southease church photographed in around 1905. Its round west tower makes it one of the more unusual of the Sussex churches.

A ROMANTIC PLACE IN WHICH TO BUY A STAMP. The thatched Post Office at Rodmell in around 1905.

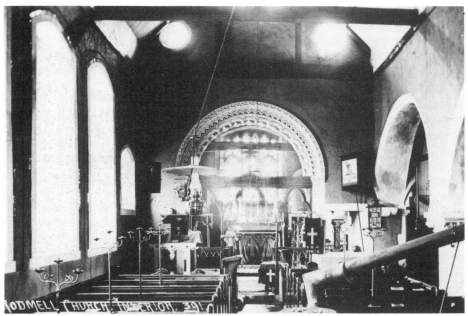

A WONDERFUL VIEW of the interior of St Peter, Rodmell. Note the hanging oil lamp, the candle sconces for the congregation and the antiquated heating in the form of an iron stove with a huge pipe leading off to the right.

A PEACEFUL SCENE AT OFFHAM photographed in around 1906. The chain link fence on the left belongs to Offham House.

A WINTER SCENE AT OFFHAM in around 1908. Note the horse which seems to be well blanketed against the cold.

Entrance, H. M. Prison, Lewes.

HOW ATTRACTIVE CAN YOU MAKE a view of a place of such forbidding aspect as Lewes Prison? The producer of this card did his best and had it delicately coloured. It was posted in 1912.

ACKNOWLEDGEMENTS

The photographs on pages 2, 77, 81 and 82 are from the Reeves Collection and they are reproduced by kind permission of the Sussex Archaeological Society and the *Sunday Times*. The photographs on pages 16 and 17 are reproduced by kind permission of Harvey's Brewery. Thanks are also due to the following:

East Sussex County Library ● Mrs E. Frost ● Mr Robert Jeeves of the Picture Postcard Saloon, Brighton ● Old Grammar School, Lewes ● Mrs R Parsons.